ORTHODOX ICON COLORING BOOK

— VOL. 7 —

20 ICONS OF NOVGOROD SCHOOL

SIMON OSKOLNIY

CONTENTS

Plate 1.
The Anunciation — 12th century
by Anonymous

Plate 2.
The Anunciation — 12th century
by Anonymous

Plate 3.
St. George — 12th century
by Anonymous

Plate 4.
St. Natalia the Martyr — 12th century
by Anonymous

Plate 5.
The Vernicle — 12th century
by Anonymous

Plate 6.
*The Dormition — 12th century
by Anonymous*

Plate 7.
St. Nicholas — 12ᵗʰ century
by Anonymous

Plate 8.
St. Nicholas — 12th century
by Anonymous

 Б ꙋ҃ы вѣ кнз҃ъ   Борисъ

19

Plate 9.
St. Boris — 12th century
by Anonymous

Plate 10.
Virgin in the Temple — 12th century
by Anonymous

Plate 11.
The Paternitas — 12th century
by Anonymous

Plate 12.
Elijah the Prophet — 12th century
by Anonymous

Plate 13.
The Apostle Thomas — 12ᵗʰ century
by Anonymous

Plate 14.
The Apostle Peter — 12th century
by Anonymous

ПР НЛЬ IА · ОА НIКОЛАЕ · IO ПРЧ

Plate 15.
*The Prophet Elijah, St.Nicholas and John the Baptist — 12th century
by Anonymous*

Plate 16.
Saints Florus, James and Laurus — 12th century
by Anonymous

Plate 17.
The Dormition — 12th century
by Anonymous

Plate 18.
Saints James, Nicholas and Ignatius — 12th century
by Anonymous

Plate 19.
The Prophet Micah — 12th century
by Anonymous

Plate 20.
The Vernicle — 12ᵗʰ century
by Anonymous

www.ingramcontent.com/pod-product-compliance
Lightning Source LLC
Chambersburg PA
CBHW081548040426
42448CB00015B/3257